Marin Mazzie , Jere Shea

VOCAL SELECTIONS FROM

PASSION

A New Musical

Music & Lyrics by
Stephen Sondheim

D0731593

Photography: Joan Marcus

© 1994 RILTING MUSIC, INC.
All rights administered by WB Music Corp.
All Rights Reserved

Marin Mazzie, Jere Shea

Marin Mazzie

Jere Shea

The Soldiers

Marin Mazzie

Donna Murphy

Marin Mazzie, Jere Shea, Donna Murphy

CONTENTS

STEPHEN SONDHEIM wrote the music and lyrics for *PASSION* (1994), *ASSASSINS* (1991), *INTO THE WOODS* (1987), *SUNDAY IN THE PARK WITH GEORGE* (1984), *MERRILY WE ROLL ALONG* (1981), *SWEENEY TODD* (1979), *PACIFIC OVERTURES* (1976), *THE FROGS* (1974), *A LITTLE NIGHT MUSIC* (1973), FOLLIES (1971, revised in London, 1987), *COMPANY* (1970), *ANYONE CAN WHISTLE* (1964), and *A FUNNY THING HAPPENED ON THE WAY TO THE FORUM* (1962), as well as the lyrics for *WEST SIDE STORY* (1957), *GYPSY* (1959), *DO I HEAR A WALTZ?* (1965) and additional lyrics for *CANDIDE* (1973). *SIDE BY SIDE BY SONDHEIM* (1976), *MARRY ME A LITTLE* (1981), *YOU'RE GONNA LOVE TOMORROW* (1983) and *PUTTING IT TOGETHER* (1992) are anthologies of his work as a composer and lyricist. For films, he composed the scores of STAVISKY (1974) and REDS (1981) and songs for DICK TRACY (Academy Award, 1990). He also wrote songs for the television production EVENING PRIMROSE (1966), co-authored the film THE LAST OF SHEILA (1973) and provided incidental music for the plays *THE GIRLS OF SUMMER* (1956), *INVITATION TO A MARCH* (1961) and *TWIGS* (1971). He won Tony Awards for Best Score for a Musical for *INTO THE WOODS, SWEENEY TODD, A LITTLE NIGHT MUSIC, FOLLIES* and *COMPANY*. All of these shows won the New York Drama Critics Circle Award, as did *PACIFIC OVERTURES* and *SUNDAY IN THE PARK WITH GEORGE*, the latter also receiving the Pulitzer Prize for Drama in 1985. Mr. Sondheim was born in 1930 and raised in New York City. He graduated from Williams College, winning the Hutchinson Prize for Music Composition, after which he studied theory and composition with Milton Babbitt. He is on the Council of the Dramatists Guild, the national association of playwrights, composers and lyricists, having served as its President from 1973 until 1981, and in 1983 was elected to the American Academy of Arts and Letters. In 1990 he was appointed the first Visiting Professor of Contemporary Theatre at Oxford University and in 1993 was a recipient of the Kennedy Center Honors.

HAPPINESS

Music and Lyrics by
STEPHEN SONDHEIM

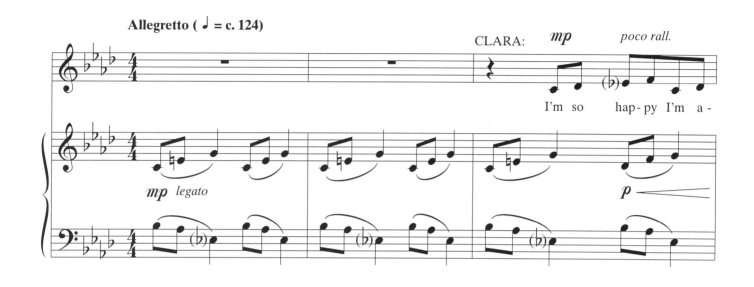

be se-duc-tive.___   How quick-ly pi-ty leads to
You pi-tied me.   How quick-ly pi-ty leads to

dim.

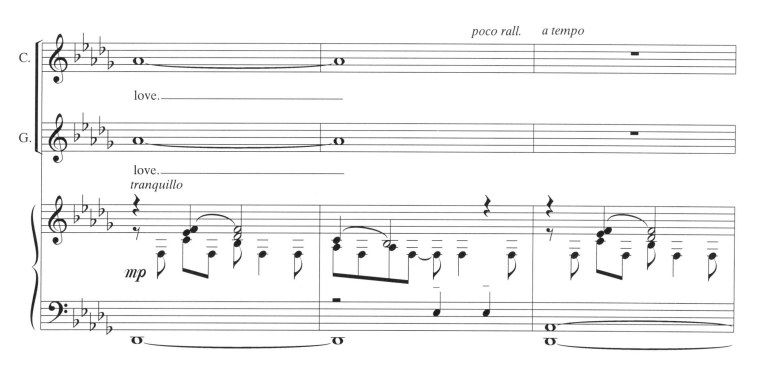

poco rall.   *a tempo*

love.___

love.___

tranquillo

mp

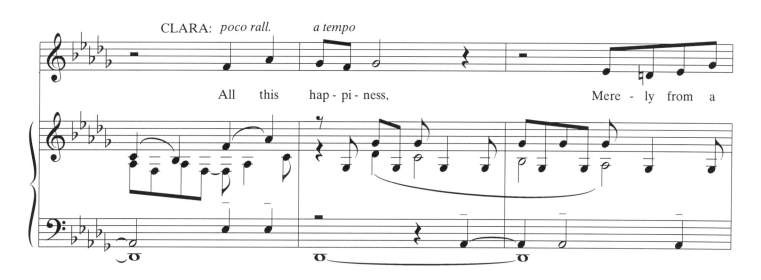

CLARA: *poco rall.*   *a tempo*

All this hap-pi-ness,   Mere-ly from a

Poco meno mosso

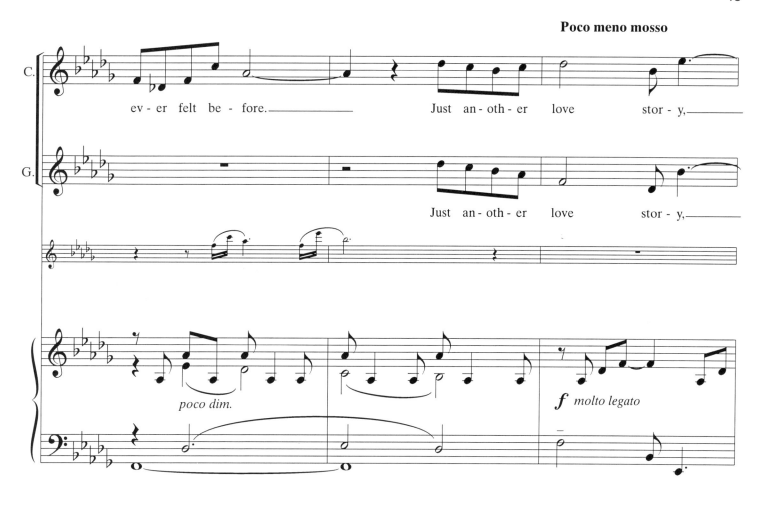

ev - er felt be - fore._____ Just an - oth - er love stor - y,_____

Just an - oth - er love stor - y,_____

poco dim. f *molto legato*

— That's what they would claim,   An - oth - er sim - ple

— That's what they would claim,   An - oth - er sim - ple

I READ

Music and Lyrics by
STEPHEN SONDHEIM

poco accel.

I know how pain-ful dreams can be Un-less you know— They're mere-ly

rall. **A la Valse**

dreams. There is a flow-er—

— Which of-fers nec-tar at the top, De-li-cious

nec-tar on the top, And bit-ter poi-son un-der-neath.

a tempo

dream be-comes an ex-pec-ta-tion.— How can I have ex-pec-ta-tions?

rall.

Look at me!— No, Cap-tain, look at me, Look at me!— I do not hope for

what I can-not have!— I do not cling to things I can-not keep! The more you

Con poco moto

poco

cling to things, The more you love them,— The more the pain you suf-fer when they're

tak - en from you._____ Ah, but if you have no ex - pec -

ta - tions, Cap - tain, you can nev - er have a dis - ap -

point - ment.

LOVE LIKE OURS

Music and Lyrics by
STEPHEN SONDHEIM

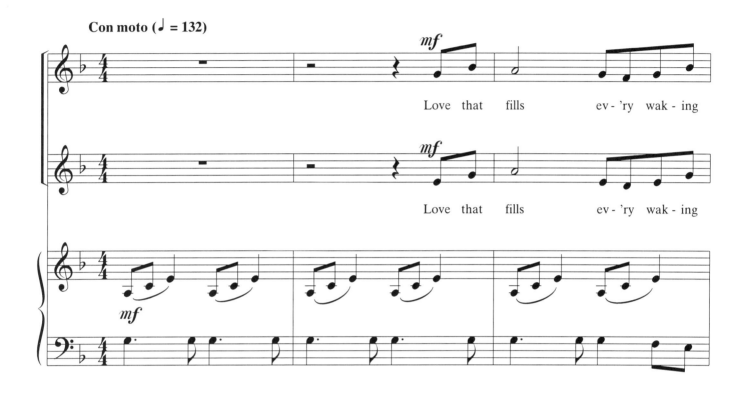

Love that fills ev - 'ry wak - ing

Love that fills ev - 'ry wak - ing

mo - ment, Love that grows ev - 'ry sin - gle day, Love that

mo - ment, Love that grows ev - 'ry sin - gle day, Love that

thinks   ev - 'ry - thing is   pure,   Ev - 'ry - thing is   beau - ti - ful,

thinks   ev - 'ry - thing is   pure,   Ev - 'ry - thing is   beau - ti - ful,

Ev - 'ry - thing is   pos - si - ble.   Love   that fus - es

Ev - 'ry - thing is   pos - si - ble.   Love   that fus - es

mf

cresc.

two in - to one, Where we think the same

two in - to one, Where we think the same

thoughts, Want the same things, Live as one, Feel as one, Breathe as one,

thoughts, Want the same things, Live as one, Feel as one, Breathe as one,

Love that shuts a-way the world,   That en-vel-ops my

Love that shuts a-way the world,   That en-vel-ops my

(L.H.)

soul,   That en-no-bles my life,   Love that

soul,   That en-no-bles my life,   Love that

dim.

floods_____ Ev-'ry liv-ing mo-ment, Love like

floods_____ Ev-'ry liv-ing mo-ment, Love like

dim.

Repeat and fade

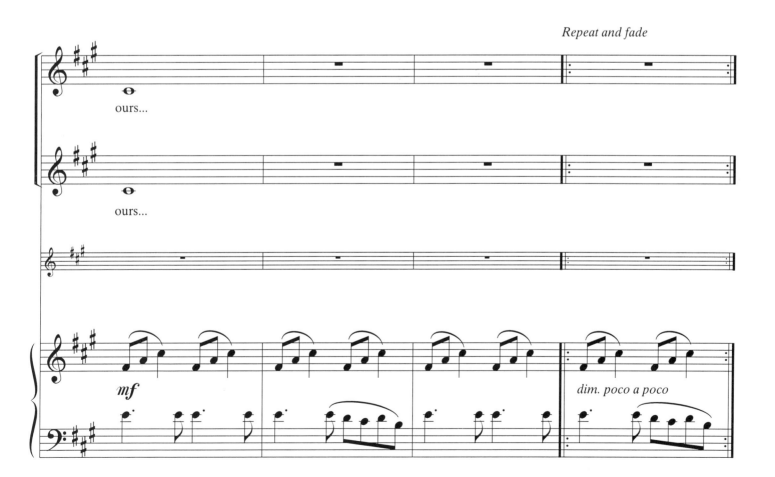

ours...

ours...

mf

dim. poco a poco

THEY HEAR DRUMS

Music and Lyrics by
STEPHEN SONDHEIM

books, Your taste, Your sen-si-tiv-i-ty, I thought you'd un-der-

stand. The oth-ers-- Well, they're all a-like. Stu-pid-i-ty is

their ex-cuse, As ug-li-ness is mine.———— But what is yours?

I've watched you from my win-dow. I saw you on the

I WISH I COULD FORGET YOU

Music and Lyrics by
STEPHEN SONDHEIM

I wish I could for-

get you, E- rase you from my mind. But ev- er since I

met you, I find I can-not leave the thought of you be - hind. That does- n't mean I

breath, As perm-a-nent as death, Im-plac-ca-ble as stone.

A love that, like a

knife, Has cut in-to a life I want-ed left a-lone.

A love I may re-

gret, But one I can't for-get.

I don't know how I

(♪ = ♪) **Tempo primo** (♩ = 104)

let you_____

So far in-side my mind.

But there you are And

there you will stay. How could I ev-er wish you a-way? I see now I was blind. And should you die to-mor-row,— An-oth-er thing I see: Your love will live in me.

LOVING YOU

Music and Lyrics by
STEPHEN SONDHEIM

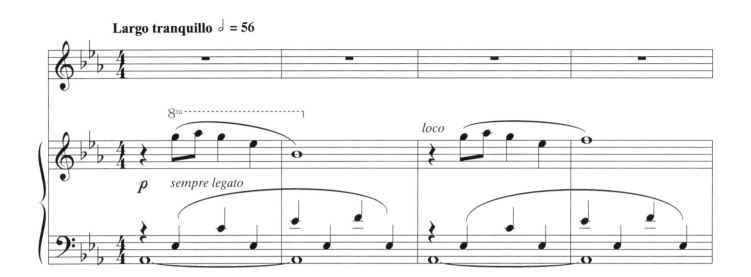

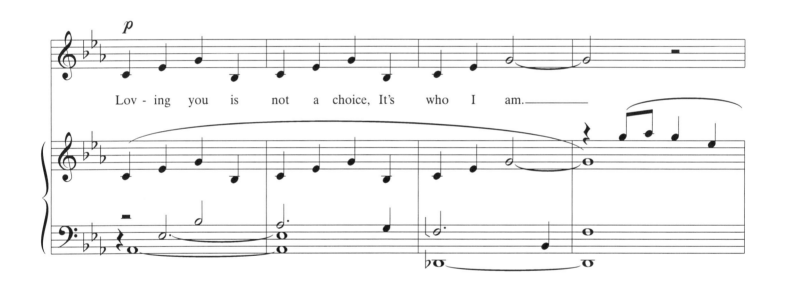

Lov - ing you is not a choice, It's who I am.

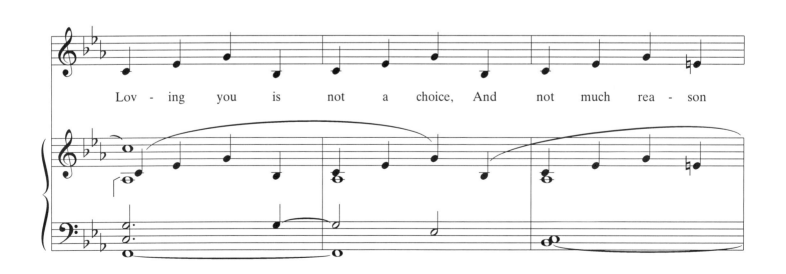

Lov - ing you is not a choice, And not much rea - son

to re- joice, But it gives me pur - pose, Gives me voice to

say to the world:_____ This is why I live.

You are why I live._____ Lov - ing you is

why I do the things I do._____

NO ONE HAS EVER LOVED ME

Music and Lyrics by
STEPHEN SONDHEIM

Con Passione (d'Amore), sempre rubato

loved me As you have, Fos - ca.

Love with - out rea - son, Love with - out mer - cy, Love with - out pride or

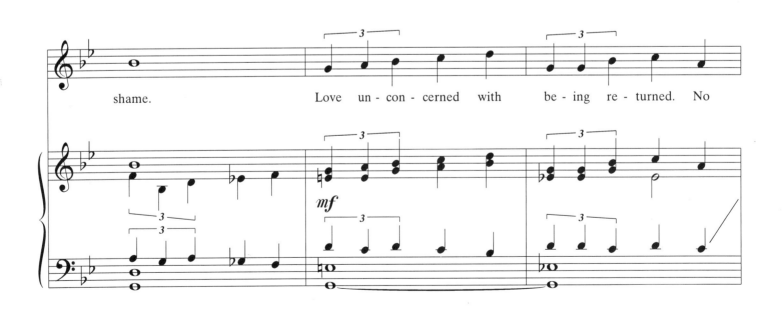

shame. Love un - con - cerned with be - ing re - turned. No

Not pret-ty or safe or eas-y, But

more than I ev-er knew. Love with-in rea-son,

Repeat and fade
(first time only)

That is-n't love. And I've learned that from you.

dim. poco a poco